FIGMENT

FIGMENT

Leila Chatti

BULL★CITY
PRESS
Durham, NC

Figment

Copyright ©2022 by Leila Chatti

Library of Congress Cataloging-in-Publication Data

Names: Chatti, Leila, 1990- author.
Title: Figment / Leila Chatti.
Description: Durham, NC : Bull City Press, [2022]
Identifiers: LCCN 2022025358 | ISBN 9781949344363 (hardcover) |
ISBN 9781949344370 (softcover)
Subjects: LCGFT: Poetry.
Classification: LCC PS3603.H37978 F54 2022 |
DDC 811/.6--dc23/eng/20220527
LC record available at https://lccn.loc.gov/2022025358

Published in the United States of America
Book design by Spock and Associates

S P O C K and
ASSOCIATES

Author photo: Aric Velbel

Published by BULL CITY PRESS
1217 Odyssey Drive
Durham, NC 27713
www.BullCityPress.com

FIGMENT

I saw you shadow of

a shadow

maybe I thought

I made you

up

a dream

I had a dream

all

but gone upon waking

Figment:

early 15c.

something invented or imagined, a myth or fable;
a feigned, invented, or imagined story, theory, etc.;
a mere product of mental invention;
something merely imagined or made up in the mind;
a fantastic notion;
deceitful practice;
false doctrine;
something that seems real but is not

amorphous
blank

belief be
lie con
ceive con
ceit

deny

dispens
able error

error ever

you a ———————
    figment
    fiction
    fantasy
    phantom

a ———————
    shiver of dream
    story someone tells me
    story I tell myself
    specter : once seen, made real

Figment

from Latin *figmentum*: something formed or fashioned, creation

not all suffering was done
to me some suffering
I wrought myself

        hours white morning poured over
        my body I didn't move I thought
        it might help to be helped I thought

I must make it clear I am helpless

faint

face   less

fabrication

false   falter
fault

fleeting
final   first

filial feeling
failure familiar

genesis

a fiction with some

truth to it : I create
        my agony I am suffering's

source and accomplice

hollow (beneath the blue hills)

morning faint
line evening black

blot into water

night night
darker streaming

in through windows I left
open

to see until there was nothing

to see

genesis   glitch   grief grief grief grief
                                           grief grief grief grief
germinal gesture   grief grief grief grief
gravid glimpse   grief grief grief grief
                                           grief grief grief grief
garnet   gore   grief grief grief grief
gray   grume   grief grief grief grief
                                           grief grief grief grief
gush   grief grief grief grief
                                           grief grief grief grief
godsent glimmer   grief grief grief grief
                                           grief grief grief grief
                                           grief grief grief grief
                                           grief grief grief grief
                                           grief grief grief grief
                                           grief grief grief grief
                 gossamer   grief grief grief grief
                                           grief grief grief grief
                                           grief grief grief grief
                                           grief grief grief grief
                                           grief grief grief grief
                                           grief grief grief grief
                                           grief grief grief grief
                                           grief grief grief grief
                                           grief grief grief grief
                                           grief grief grief grief
                                           grief grief grief grief
                                           grief grief grief grief
                                           grief grief grief grief
                                           grief grief grief grief
                                           grief grief grief grief

gone

faint

the image   haze

                        of the interior

gray like   the color

                        of nothing

light   unable to be held

            in the eye   featureless

day   a blur   how long

            did I stand   there

            did I stand

            it

                        shhh shhh

poured   before

swoon

13

haltingly   hollowed
hallowed
hallucination

happening hardly
hidden hard

ship
harmed   harbor
harbinger

hysterical
              hush hush
hope   hurt   hellish
holding

illegible ill
usion ill
usory image
imagined in
conclusive in
carnadine ink
ling imp
ending in
curable

if if if

January	June	July
January	jelly	jewel
keel	kneel	knell
kindle	kinder	kin
keep	keep	keep
leak	lack	luck
less	less	lost
long	longing	lingering
lull	lull	aby
bye	*bye*	*bye*

smudge

of dusk
the night

slow at first

then steadily, steadily

all there was

mothered
made   mad
madder matter
mattered

I resolved to pass you enact you   past
I thought if I could render you   memory
then next I could forget

troubling heaven ·
                                complications
        of cloud

sun dropped a drop
red red inter
posed between
now   the dark future

nothing
nestling
nowhere
needless
negation no
negotiation

I cried

      thick blank tears
      in the gray light of no time

      a mistake
      a mistake
      to think

      you nothing nothing
      is nothing

O!

O omen
O otherworld

object
O permanence
please   O pleas
O passing
pulp palpable
pain

O!
O!

O proof
O quiver
O ruin

                    root

from the root *dheigh- :
to form, build

as if from dough from clay

fictile   I formed

you I didn't know   before

I did it   what I was

capable of   *fainéant*

little   do nothing

hurt   no one

but myself   an effigy

I could not bear   to burn

all the way   down

I thought   I was no good

a fiction   someone told me

not you   one I loved

before   how I suffered

before I knew you   how

I suffered   after

oh my   one good thing

undone   now

you somewhere   I imagine

like paradise

23

seen:

shadow

sac

red

secret

safekept

subsequent scarlet

sentimental

sediment

sanguine

sheets

saw   no   gram

speck

something

[*spectacle*]

self suddenly

stranger

terrible terrible   tenderness

    twinge   then

             there   *there*

                  torrent

          thither   *thither*

threnody
    thrashing the trees

subjunctive mood

if you were I would see you
seeing the rain I see you see
if it were raining if you were
within view and new still
surprised by the world seen
through the rain the world
blurs if you were more than
anything I would wish you
here to see it miniature
in each drop a world
dropped from me no one
knew you see I kept you
to myself like everything
I love you see how I know
nothing but want
to show you look the sky
teeming if I were with you
in the world we'd be in it

uncarry unsuckle unrock uncoo
unswaddle uncradle unsleep unwake
unbabble uncry unsing unlullaby
unopen unclose unhand uneye
unwish unanswer unexpect unknow
unroot ungrow untouch unlove
unbear unbearable unbe unwas

you a ————
    notion
    nothing
    nobody
    no

vanished

vocabulary

~~visible~~
~~viable~~
~~visceral~~
void

visitant

violently
violently

weeks wept
weak   writhing

            window white, wet

without warning
weeks

wordless

            witness: woman

whose wound within
wrong   *world*

who whispered *why why why why why*

an idea I came up

with you beyond harm

who would know

days of light days

brightness erased the world

in the tub a life

time I floated like an idea

I came up heaving stunned

words only   half gathered

in cold unrelenting sun

from far away a voice
asking how am I

                    feeling oh I say I am feeling

          (   )

   just fine

you came

           from zephyr
           from ether
                  into neither
           never

     out of nothing
     into

xx   xy

you   *you-who*—

yesterwas

yondermost

you   yes you

Zeitlang   زمنا

figment of speech
when I speak

of you I conjure you

    inkling

      in ink in language
      you are here you are
      given shape shaped for
      you a space
              held

now you in the story

    faint yes brief
    yes but here

figure of my imagination

NOTE

Figment owes a debt of gratitude to Jean Valentine, whose words and silences helped me discover my own. *"words only/ half gathered"* is borrowed from her poem "Embryo."

ABOUT THE AUTHOR

Leila Chatti is the author of the full-length collection *Deluge* (Copper Canyon Press, 2020), winner of the 2021 Levis Reading Prize, the 2021 Luschei Prize for African Poetry, and longlisted for the 2021 PEN Open Book Award, and the chapbooks *The Mothers* (Slapering Hol Press), *Ebb* (New-Generation African Poets), and *Tunsiya/Amrikiya*, the 2017 Editors' Selection from Bull City Press. She is the recipient of a Pushcart Prize, grants from the National Endowment for the Arts, the Barbara Deming Memorial Fund, and the Helene Wurlitzer Foundation of New Mexico, and fellowships and scholarships from the Fine Arts Work Center in Provincetown, the Wisconsin Institute for Creative Writing, the Tin House Writers' Workshop, the Kenyon Review Writers Workshop, the Sewanee Writers' Conference, the Frost Place Conference on Poetry, the Key West Literary Seminars, Dickinson House, and Cleveland State University, where she was the inaugural Anisfield-Wolf Fellow in Writing and Publishing. She is the Grace Hazard Conkling Writer-in-Residence at Smith College and lives and writes in Massachusetts and the Midwest.

ALSO BY LEILA CHATTI

Tunsiya/Amrikiya

Ebb

Deluge

The Mothers: Poems in Conversation & A Conversation
(with Dorianne Laux)

Yellow Dog
(an imprint of Great Plains Publications)
1173 Wolseley Avenue
Winnipeg, MB R3G 1H1
www.greatplains.mb.ca

Great Plains Publications gratefully acknowledges the financial support provided for its publishing program by the Government of Canada through the Canada Book Fund; the Canada Council for the Arts; the Province of Manitoba through the Book Publishing Tax Credit and the Book Publisher Marketing Assistance Program; and the Manitoba Arts Council.

Design & Typography by Relish New Brand Experience
Printed in Canada by Friesens

Library and Archives Canada Cataloguing in Publication

Title: You don't have to die in the end : a novel / by Anita Daher.
Names: Daher, Anita, 1965- author.
Identifiers: Canadiana (print) 20200165216 | Canadiana (ebook) 20200165232 | ISBN 9781773370439 (softcover) | ISBN 9781773370453 (Kindle) | ISBN 9781773370446 (EPUB)
Classification: LCC PS8557.A35 Y69 2020 | DDC jC813/.6—dc23

ENVIRONMENTAL BENEFITS STATEMENT

Great Plains Publications saved the following resources by printing the pages of this book on chlorine free paper made with 100% post-consumer waste.

TREES	WATER	ENERGY	SOLID WASTE	GREENHOUSE GASES
11	930	5	39	4,890
FULLY GROWN	GALLONS	MILLION BTUs	POUNDS	POUNDS

Environmental impact estimates were made using the Environmental Paper Network Paper Calculator 40. For more information visit www.papercalculator.org.

Canadä

FSC
www.fsc.org
MIX
Paper from responsible sources
FSC® C016245